Praise for
La La Landia: A Journey Through my Frontera CD Shuffle

This is a book that feels like a welcome home to me, a dance made out of *the limbo of lenguajes*, a home to my pocha mind that straddles memories of old school Timbiriche amidst the protective and complex spirit of Moon Mother, a place where the faces of family members, asoleadas, muertas, y enamoradas carry hidden landscapes, histories, and cuentos that are cast into poems, into poetry that remembers and honors la vida entre los bailes, los desayunos con Welo, y los balazos. Here, we are immersed in the ropaje of the borderlands formed by dichos, música, traditions, and wisdom that warm and teach us tenderly amid scenes of grief, loss, and violence, and that fortify the future of la la landia with hope as we *wrap our senses/ around [the] small, sheltered world* inside the sacred and ancient sustenance of morning with un tamal recalentado.

—**Natalia Treviño**, author of *VirginX* and *Lavando La Dirty Laundry*

The poems of *La La Landia* by Priscilla Celina Suárez are of life on the southern border crisscrossing cultures and generations, time traveling in stories and song, steeped in love, family, and memory. There is music and heart in these words. Suárez writes "their stories are like a trance / we as offspring cannot escape," her ancestors' lives and the mysteries we all live with make this collection breathe with energy, goodwill, laughter, and kindness.

—**Angie Trudell Vasquez**, MFA
Madison, Wisconsin Poet Laureate 2020-2024

La La Landia is a borderlands feast for the senses: "Chocolate Abuelita with a tinge of canela," a taco stand speaker blaring banda music, code switching tongues, hearts bursting con nostalgia for a place and time that seems to evaporate cómo las aguas del río. Suárez casts familiar characters through a new lens, one tainted by policies that separate children from their mothers, by the violence that disappears truth tellers, a beloved primo, a young woman who was once a friend. Here Llorona weeps "into the many directions / a child can flow." Here the poet offers consejos to our younger selves, holds up las cosas que hicimos por pendeja, a reminder that even when we know better, we don't always do better, especially for ourselves. And still, here we are. Here Priscilla Celina Suárez is. And we're all the better for it.

—**Michelle Otero**, Albuquerque Poet Laureate 2018-2020
author of *Malinche's Daughter* and *Bosque: Poems*

La La Landia:

A JOURNEY THROUGH
MY FRONTERA CD SHUFFLE

La La Landia:

A JOURNEY THROUGH MY FRONTERA CD SHUFFLE

FLOWERSONG
PRESS

poetry by

Priscilla Celina Suárez

FLOWERSONG
PRESS

FlowerSong Press
Copyright © 2022 by Priscilla Celina Suárez
ISBN: 978-1-953447-51-7
Library of Congress Control Number: 2022932200

Published by FlowerSong Press
in the United States of America.
www.flowersongpress.com

Cover Art and Design by Priscilla Celina Suarez
Set in Adobe Garamond Pro

NOTICE: SCHOOLS AND BUSINESSES
FlowerSong Press offers copies of this book at quantity discount with bulk
purchase for educational, business, or sales promotional use. For information,
please email the Publisher at info@flowersongpress.com.

Dedicated to my parents, for teaching me the art of listening to cuentos. And for all the music and dancing and love.

Acknowledgements

I have so much gratitude for my gente and the generous support they have shown me while working on this project. It has taken an entire community to put this book together.

I have to start by thanking my papito, Luis Armando Suárez, and my mami (QEPD), Sylvia Suárez de la Garza, for the road trips down memory lane and for being the root of my storytelling ventures. My brothers, Tim (QEPD) and Louie, and sisters, Melissa and Jessica, for being a part of these memories I share and for embracing me as I am.

Special thanks to my amiga del alma, Esther del Carmen Garcia, for her invaluable feedback when selecting the poetry to include in this collection, for encouraging me to release it into the world, and for coming up with the title of this book. So much gratitude for mis amigos Sara P. Montoya, Anthony Luna, and Angel S. Salinas for the random discussions and support throughout this process.

Many abrazos to all the mentors and compadres *(and there are many)* I have been lucky to come across in the Valle's arts and poetry scene from both sides of the frontera. In particular, to my crew from the Chocholichex Writing Collective (Rodney Gomez, Nayelli Barrios, César L. de León, Celina A. Gomez, and Isaac Chavarría) for the chisme, the laughter, and the guidance when workshopping several of these poems. And, finally, a huge shout out to FlowerSong Press and the Vidaurres for giving this book a home.

Versions of several of the poems included in this collection have appeared in the following publications (as well as a few others not listed because I am so disorganized): *The Monitor, Antologia Oficial Festival Internacional de Poesia Latinoamericana, The Windward Review, Fright: An Anthology by the McAllen Public Library Writing Circle, Bad Hombres and Nasty Women, Interstice (South Texas College), Along the River III: Voices from the Rio Grande, Juventud!: Growing Up in the Border, Stories and Poems, Boundless, The Maiz Chronicles,* and *Bordersenses.*

CAUTION

This book was written by a pocha and will intentionally
include a lot of Tex-Mex spanglish and made up words. If you
read this book, please don't be annoyed by my pocha tongue.
It is my language and I made a choice.

Contents

III. STORIES AND HEIRLOOMS

IV. LAS LLORONAS SING BALADAS AND VALSES

I

Just Past the Perimeter

"Los árboles nos unen."
— popular Mexican dicho

Una Tarde in the
Dentista's Waiting Room

Tocan una canción
de Ramón Ayala y Sus Bravos del Norte.
Nada me importa… I hear him
croon from the speakers outside
a Las Flores[1] dentista's office. I stare
> outside the glass doors
> into a busy world
> where sombreros and bootleg CDs
> block my view from the dusty & dirty road.

I hear Lucerito's voice
but can't quite make out the song.
I smell the scent of a Dr.'s office
making me nauseous
with the fear of needles.
> I close my eyes for a few seconds -
> and in those seconds
> I swallow Ramón's music
> with the sincerity of the gente
> making up this gabachita's corrido.

a bit tejana, rancherita.
a bit hip hop, pop.
a bit classical, antigüita.
but a lot, a lot Tex-Mex fresa[2].
> Tesoro. My favorite word in Ramon's
> vocabulary. *Tesoro,* I repeat
> and think back to an overload of faces.

My tesoritos, songwriters de mi alma.
The air-con's vent
throws me cool air
on this typical afternoon
of asoleadas and aguas frescas.

Mis motivos are,
no matter where I go,
to carry this feeling
of being home. Of the love
I still carry for people I've
loved and lost, buried and died for -
to carry them
as they've carried me.

Quereme

para el Tío Esteban

¿Qu'en la que're? me pregunta
el Tío Esteban, *¿qu'en?*

¡Pos, tú tío!

The cabrito roasting on the chimney
as the odor of fresh-baked tamales
and the llantos del Grupo Bronco
swam from inside this wonderful
and familiar Reynosa home.

> My tío - apa's primo - is a clear
> example of amor de familia;
> unconditional, disregarding the
> distance and bonds of time.

It is like the anillo
a distant bruja aunt
presented me with -
a woman I'd heard
about and feared all my life.
But with one shared laugh, I knew.

> Or like Catarino's football Sundays and
> Univision mornings in Michigan -
> so far from home
> but con familía I'd never met.

It was like
meeting la Tía Tomasa
again, or el long lost primo Chuy,
or like the need of meeting

the abuelita I never met...
      I'd whisper to her *Quereme.*
      Quereme.

Welo's Mustache

in memory of Abuelito Florentino

Tonta ladeada, he teased
the first time I noticed his lack of a mustache.
I was eighteen and cancer
had kicked him in the lungs.

Nothing on his face
but the question of haggard wrinkles
running in contrast to the lines of my palm
and marking his sixty-some years of life.

Before crossing the river
he never imagined borders
would embrace the limbo of lenguajes
or that an imaginary lingo
would someday spill from his mouth
and stray on the neat wisps of his barba.

I see history and lineages
spit and acknowledgment
humanity and labels
when I stare at a sepia portrait of him
from that era.

His auburn beard and sharp eyes
a piercing resemblance to
the welo whose creases were more profound
after he lost his lifelong companion.

A mustache that walked away
as a reminder life is short
and although a sombrero could
conceal his missing hairlines,

a palm would never
hide his running mouth.

Cabrona, pela'o, descara'o!

If I had inherited the illustrations
his lively vocabulary painted and
if foul words came naturally to me
maybe I wouldn't have been
so quick to discard my own whiskers.

Maybe I would have needed them to adorn
my lips as I puckered to spill
poems full of reputations that mark
my brown skin and pocha tongue.

My welo's reputation transitioned
with every era of his mustache.

Before it ran away to an early death
he wore it as a neatly trimmed
salt-colored beauty on his upper lip.

The landscape on his face
dry as clay from the asoleadas of sunny
summerlike winters in las labores de Las Milpas[1]
rows of ripe sugar canes
falling against his peeling
worn fingers that meshed
with this land of ranchos and colonias.

[1] *Was previously a colonia in South Texas*

cántame una canción de Dios

in memory of Abuelito Eduardo

cántame una canción de Dios, me dice mi abuelo
as he waits his turn
to hear me sing his song. spirits teasing us
all around
while I try to fasten into a tune.
      una de Jóse Alfredo Jiménez, or Javier Solís,
      I think – but no, él quiere una canción de Dios.
una de rock & roll, he whispers,
from between '50 & '54. what the girls
used to sing back when we went up North.

his brown hands are holding mine. his presence is there
before me but in his state,
he's thousands of miles away.
      I think back to all the songs
      I've heard before. I think back to all the songs
we've sung together. I think back twenty years
so that in my memory, I can find the tune
he's sure to find comfort in. But, I've never
thought of it as a canción
I would sing to this man ready to let
everything, absolutely everything, go.

I don't want the world to know
I can't fight the tears
straining to be heard
as I sing him his song. I feel he's
not listening, but he sings. he sings.

and he hears
every tear in every word
with every moment

I don't want the world to forget.
      because with this song,
      I understand. and I feel broken
      in knowing who I am
      is not because of me, but
      because of this man
      and our family
we sing una canción de Dios for.

From Abuelita's Dichos

dedicated to the abuelitas in my life

Abuelita was a wonderwall of dichos.
Some picosos, otros sabios,
and many I could never quite figure out.

She would tell us, her granddaughters,
Cuando alguien juzgue tu camino,
préstale tus zapatos.

How did she know
there would be days
our voice would ask for permission to be heard?
That the details of our world
would be a map no GPS could guide us to?
Or how we would be told to start over
before the starting even began?

Mi'jita de mi vida, she'd advise after seeing us
tread obstacles, *lo.que no te mate te hace más fuerte,*
más dura, más fría, más mala, y más guapa.

Wisdom she fed us with her dichos
in a means to revolt
against her years of silence.

Las palabras se las lleva
el viento, she'd whisper, with a hope
she'd cast us outside that box
of stereotypes so
we'd walk the walk
against invisible borders.

She collected strips of dichos

not knowing she was sowing bows of honor,
believing that *Ausencia al más amigo presto*
le pone en olvido.

But look at her now,
word by word,
a poem spoken from my mouth.

Maybe I can hear her humming Infante's
Yo soy quien soy y no me parezco a naidien…
when I doubt the two cents I choose to give.

Because though I doubt
the path I have taken,
it was mine – and only mine –
to take.

Dichos become dangerous
when used against doubt, as
I learned from that huatosa[1] viejita
wrapped in layers of ropaje and rebozos
as she reminded us *quien con lobos anda*
a aullar se enseña.

Y míranos.

Look at us.

A family of sorts
with the comadres we find
in every journey of life.

I look around my communities
and can visualize
Abuelita's favorite dicho:
Dime con quién andas
y te diré quién eres.

In a room of nietas and abuelitas to come
I can exhale amidst an ocean of dreams

and consejos that bond
each and every one of us.

We are bearers of her wonderwall of dichos
as we remember to take her example
of living life by her motto:
No cuentes tus días,
haz que tus días cuenten.

Pepe Who Didn't Know Death Was His to Take

a dragon tattoo on his left arm
shifts into place
as Pepe relaxes his shoulders
when he sees
how I notice him.

in his eyes
chismes strain to live
and with fire, he speaks
as if he has never been heard before.

desire in me runs
to smooth his greasy black hair down –
tousled by thoughts of how for sure
this visit would come.
I consider pulling at his chin
when he rubs his goatee
and his sunglasses fall out of place.

but it is in the glaze
of his eyes – white, all white.

he realizes we never met in life
when I startle
with his two-step advance.
but despite my sudden shock
and awareness, he asks me
why I recognize him.

The talk, the chismes,
the people we share, I whisper,
is how we meet in this moment's dream.

I strain to hear his thoughts

and wonder if Pepe
is genuinely the angry cholo
he was infamous to be.

his blackened lips
speak words wiser.

her tug-of-war

in memory of Nana Toña

the ages that passed
somewhere
had turned   into miles
separating her hopes
from that of before
        and the much before

not that it took away
        her love
from what was
to what had become

my viejita
had transformed
into a blanket of stories and lullabies

a blanket of an indígena
and a mejicana
and now
a tejana from somewhere else

a tug-of-war
that pulls her this way   and that
that way
        and there
        there
and over here

and it has
for a long, long time

no hopes

can cause such pity
unless she surpassed them
      and gave those

a part of her   to a piece of us
as though we be her children
and the blood she has carried

if it means something,
I am more a part of her
than what blood
I truly carry

I go on Crossing Rivers

for Angel

I go on crossing rivers
not knowing how to stay still
or let go of the pasts haunting me

poco a poquito
the drabby wind fluttered
to lift the roots at the depth
of this blind heart

when I think of you
and you appear
I feel how you've
set fire to the comfortable, safe
haven I'm used to

no matter how life changes
your essence challenges me
as I go on crossing rivers
not knowing how to stay still

you've watched me fall
at times when
no one else would notice,
only you

the echoes of your soothing
arms have fixed me
and you, without a clue

I've taken breaths
trying to let go…
and as I was drowning

poco a poquito
here I've crossed those fears
to find how all along
I've loved you

We Came to La Frontera in 1947

we came to la frontera in 1947
me dicen mis abuelos

él es del cumbre
y ella de la ciudad

bruto como tú, me dicen
alegre y sin razón

reservada como tú, me dicen
tranquila y olvidada de la vida

eres como las vacas
de Gregorio Cortez, me dicen
más de acá
y sin inquietud o sospechas
sobre la abuja del reloj

y nosotros viejitos
como los caballos de la Kiñena[1]
so sought after
even Chente Fernández and Pepe Aguilar
compran sus caballos allí

pero a ti
¿cómo compararte con caballos?
sí ni las reatas de lazar
can keep you from running crazy

tu piensas que tu vida
es como el maguey
la ordeñas todos los días
para sacarle su miel

no te das cuenta
de lo que te pide la luna

no como los abuelos
que viven por dudas

[1]Refers to the region of Kingsville, TX

tan loca

he waited for me, a few hours or so,
as I dug my nails
beneath the rocks
      they eased as I dug
      and I found what I had been searching for.
ya no te quiero, I tell him
but even my voice doesn't believe me –
      ay!
I flick the dirt from beneath my nails
and then look up at the absent stars
and then I look to him
      so he smiles that teasing grin
      I hate a million times ten
¿tu no me quieres? it asks me
adorable, adorable, adorable –
      ay.
ya no te quiero.

jamas will anticipation

I keep   crossing fronteras in anticipation
of a river that can make me chingona -
but no distance   is ever enough

I have no such guts of rebellion
most hociconas are born with
and neither is my rage a mountain
of cries or challenging duels

I find
        I do not
                move
                        mountains

do not judge my rage
because of its silence

I keep   crossing fronteras in circles
with espinazos you can only feel, not see
mírame with neat trenzas
and a confident stride -
        pero even that does not lead me from
        this worrisome path of la mala vida

        jamas
si no se puede
        si se puede
si no se puede

they used to call you
the silent cordillera
with your strumming a dream
broken hearts are made of

jamas will you be again

it is faith in you
to be   broken
          piece   by   piece
and not the bones
                          nor the thought
                                                                of letting go
can make a blessing change

my body
separates   from
                              my mind
and it is yet not enough

anticipation the rebeldía
we have brought forth
with this consent
                                                            to jamas let go

The Phone Rang

in memory of Abuelito Eduardo

after hanging up on the goodbyes
of my abuelo, El Colorín,
I heard myself talking
to the memories in my heart.

I want to be free
and leave with whoever
will let me run loose
but when one loves, as free as they
say one should feel, I am never really so.

I want to dream in black & white
and not feel the breezes
color mixes in
but without the tinted mirrors
of this world
I would only wonder
about the in-betweens.

I want to run to an ejido
in the sierras
and find the bones of his body
but his bones would've been buried
and his spirit would've followed
me so far along.

I want to know how to hang up on him
and never wait by the phone
wondering if abuelo will call home
      but without a landline
      how would he reach me
      and ask me to water the plants?

and ask me to kiss my abuela goodnight?
and remind me to nurture the birds
on their journey north, or south?
and ask me
about life after his departure?

La La Landia and Blues

"Al mal tiempo, buena cara."
— popular Mexican dicho

Invisible Borders
in memory of the frontera that was

Dime con quien andas y te dire
quien eres. It is a dicho as natural
as the next thought.

In our culture
your roots are your ties,
but they are not your future –
at least, that's how it feels.
> Tell me who I am y te dire
> I am confused. The holidays
> of jumping culturas
> have transitioned.

Nímodo.

I made excuses. I confused
myself with theories. I jumped
from skin to shell
with my lenguajes –
that's what my borders gave me. Infinite
roads of luck and legends.

> Leyendas – that's what my sobrinos
> know of our frontera roots. Rooted,
> in all honesty.

That absence of confusion will be
their invisible border. Not knowing
what it feels like
to be uprooted – not knowing
lenguajes consist of more than
what you can hear.

I listen to their voices and
understand
they know only of belonging
while I struggle
to pertain –
invisible borders
shutting
and keeping me out.

Nímodo.

A Newspaper Headline

I.

Dad shakes open the newspaper
so the headline
faces me / another cartel drug boss
in custody en este la'o / a standoff
and a conspiracy / it goes in circles
but those handcuffed hands
are of a lifeline that doesn't end with a cell.

I need family and friends
to be angry as I am / maybe they are
and perhaps I overreact sometimes /
we as a raza have overcome many obstacles together /
that headline is uncertain.

II.

"mass grave" found in San Fernando[1].
San, San, San, San, San.

III.

I've heard my community's voice
in the words of a frontera blogger / things we'd never
say in public / we are never really safe
from the inseguridad / uncertain
of the truths / rumors
reach our ears / even en este la'o.

IV.

Driving home a few days later / at a bus stop
I make eye contact with a viejita / she doesn't smile
doesn't look away

I see those eyes when I look in the rearview mirror /
I see those eyes on the face of a journalist
gone missing in Tijuana / I see those eyes in two portraits
included in the obituaries page / I see those eyes when I pray
to God / I see them as I write this.

---

[1] *In 2011, 193 bodies were recovered from mass graves in San Fernando,
Tamaulipas. Most were the remains of Central American migrants.*

A Taste of Dirt

when the girl died
there was no coffin
to carry her out
of this world.
she died
       tasting the dirt
         she'd never be buried in
         but consumed by.
she'd never
remember her name
or this absurd
loneliness that became
her lucky path.

Bendita.

the girl left no
bloody stains
where the flames turned
her to ash
       and her breasts
carried no memory
where her children
nestled their head -
       in those days,
       Bendita.

a year later
she is desaparecida -
dead like the thousand
before her,
       but not so.

Bendita.

her ashes stinging
her lover´s eyes
like steam from
a burning grave
      and fuming like
dry ice against
      a turned cheek.

she is impatient
no more. she is simply

Bendita.

Reynosa Huaraches

In the braving summer heat of 101°
a shredding sombrero fans at his face,
mosquitoes swaddled around him.
> broken tiles of concrete are no
> nuisance to his heels
> as he walks on one of the dirtiest
> streets of Reyno-town[1].
Streaming from the speaker
of a taquito stand
sounds a tune he most enjoys
shuffling his feet to...
con estos huaraches que traigo yo,
muchas veces te e venido a ver.

His 3-year-old voice trembles
when his father yells
for him, and instantly knows it is too late.
Emilianito's trembling hands are
accustomed to the colder than cold
feeling because of the blocks of ice
he scraped; he didn't even cry
in the heat of the moment
as he let go, as he let go...
con estos huaraches que traigo yo,
muchas veces te e venido a ver.

Black SUV's stroll the streets
near the Calle del Taco[2]
where the world stopped
most recently - but
despite the firing grenades,
work never ceases to end.
tu no me quieres corresponder

y eso aquí dentro me va doler.

Emiliano Sr. sits by that curb
across the street
from where bullets swerved,
cuddling stray huaraches
as soldados tear him away
from his niño's body...
tu no me quieres corresponder
y eso aquí dentro me va doler.

Maybe time will fly by
as did the moments of his last breath.
Maybe a journalist will be
brave enough to mark
his death in printed ink,
but we'd all doubt it...
estos huaraches que traigo yo
pronto se me van a desgastar.

With a set of Santa María's
breathing out of spectating neighbors,
nothing is as it should be
but as it is
with this child's fresh face
spilling tears, not his own.

his life gone,
and gone his life...
estos huaraches que traigo yo
pronto se me van a desgastar.

It won't be days
before a makeshift cross
made from scraps and pieces
pierces the earth
stained and marked by his youth.

He had shifted his feet
in one last dance...

y yo descalso voy a quedar
por estas tierras a caminar.

Unos que otros
se persinan,
crossing about in their huaraches
through this ghost town
of fried fish con lime y aguas frescas.

Scrambling about in fear
of these new times
in the braving summer heat of 101°.

y yo descalso voy a quedar
por estas tierras a caminar.

[1] *Slang for Reynosa, Tamaulipas*
[2] *Street in Reynosa nicknamed by locals for its abundance of taquito stands*

wicked – her secret words

her secret words

they glare at me
and sneer within
how I am wicked

more wicked now
to opt to live in sin

I never hear her
say the words
but I know, I must know
she is displeased

I come from a long line of sinners
el mal hecho is in my blood

bad habits, they became me

this pobre m'ija is an ingrate
to her devotion

wicked as the women of my blood
full of mal hechos
and so far from God's

her secret words

I never hear her
say the words
but I know, I must know
I am not the saint
she thought me

somewhere beneath my open stare
me bendice
with her secret words

and I know, I must know

I am too wicked
to be the woman
she meant me to be

Generation Bang Bang*

you look at me thru
a sideways glance
      your hand holding your wela's
      but you don't wave goodbye.
you are always on my mind, little boy
siempre en mi mente.
hasta luego, muchachito de mi alma,
I whisper
and hug you with my words
as I walk out the door.

the tension is heavy

I feel it, you feel it
because our hopes
are only our hopes.
      three weeks away from
      your mother's disappearance
      and you without knowing
      what it means she's gone.
you cry for your father
when his legacy was you
and you can't comprehend
how your life has begun.

your eyes are sad
because wela's weak spirit
gestures to you
      how wrong things have gone.
your tíos and tías
come from near and far
walking into the harmony
of these days gone long

disrupting the peace
of a mourning household
grieving for the probabilities
your parents are no longer yours.

¿quién sabe? what happens
and how many corpses
your tíos will have to see
before they can claim
what is yours
but not fairly so.
quisiera decir algo
to help you cope with what's to come
but I cannot make promises
when I dread the signs
aiming from all angles.

this time of peace
if there was ever any at all
was short-lived for you.

for you who has heard
the wailing of bullets, sirens, and
shouts, warning you to duck.

for you who has witnessed
torched automobiles and
homes set ablaze from next door.

for you who has jumped
from one TV station to the next
craving to see a cartoon
instead of war infested news.

for you who might always
live to wonder
what torture your parents
have gone through
and whether they can be
revenged from fault.

what makes me stand here
and wish words were actions
stronger than panic
is your situation
not being anything special.
      you are a statistic
      of how life has become
from that side of
      this borderland we share.

According to Borderland Beat, it is a term (coined by Francisco Benavides) that refers to children currently growing up in Mexico's violent society

wish I were more political

wishes revolve and in
this world of mine
I live in - it is far, far
from what you've heard.
        people like me,
        we live comfortably
        with eyes shut
        and listening. lies, lies there.
        we know
        just how those lies
        come forth.
politicos, periodistas, students,
mistaken identities -
        I've known more
        than one of each to die.
known them, loved them,
but not quite like them
when my world
is shut to theirs.
        people like me,
        we live comfortably
with eyes shut
        and listening.

Loca Carel

tan tan tan

her heels tripping
ears listening
heads turning
checking her out

and then her hands go
            in the air.
        up
    up,
up,

the strums Mana tunes
in this musica internaciónal club
are the tan, tan, tans of her heartbeats.

loca fresa
all dressed up and provoking
riots intended to distract
attention towards her.

no hay palabras
that compare to her modish slang
as car doors open and club doors close
and single sweet lies become a search
in her weekend excursion
from her real world
        to this surreal fantasy.

Carel was the queen of La Zona Dorada[1]
hitting the night scene
with her pricey pair of black heels

her fragrant perfume
lingering as her hair inhaled
the cigarette smoke wrapping about her.

I imagine feeling her hand's warmth
as she hurried me thru the VIP crowd -
her destination always being to get
to the bottle of vodka.

loca fresa as she was
when old school Timbiriche songs hit the airwaves:
o sea, beyby, toca madera
porque este antro que se pone requetebueno
y nada que ver con tu vida de mosca.
o sea ponte lista
porque se te acaba ese look de huelemoles.

Loca de remate as her hair spun
and we dazed off into a secret world of
fist-pumping, eyes closing to the thuds
of international pop paces
and the unity of our offbeat singing.

Her hand reaching for mine
as she led me
to our dance floor throne.

tan, tan, tan
I hear in the distance
and sometimes imagine it could be her

as if this year passed and gone
were simply a bad dream
without her missing whereabouts or without
closed borders that have taken
many others I've known

                                          away

into the abyss of frontera mysteries.

Carel danced many times
with the fever of lost dreams
a little too gone for modesty.

but I wonder
whether he led her away by hand

it shouldn't matter…
o sea, thinking things through
doesn't explain when by that time
we had many distances separating our identities.

I read poems now
when I borrowed songs before
our identities split into two.

no quise detenerla
when we grew apart

and without a body
and without a trace,
there is no reason
not to imagine.

¹For generations, was an entertainment district in
Reynosa lined with night clubs

Milagros

beneath the desert sun
and with some trouble
I wait on Milagros
       feet twitching
       in the frying sand
       I wish for her to come
       and wish she not
the mirror of anxiety
lifts my head and
pulses in this loss as
the glare stares me down
       Milagros defeats my purpose
       struggle bites at my ribs
and I could almost
feel her come to me

but Milagros
is the womb of the dead –
she comes out of nowhere
with no pledge to pry

Milagros
is a barrier between
this life and   that death

a barrier between him and me

Milagros
stands between us
       my eyes darken
       with a blackest despise
       and if it isn't her fault
then she need not exist at all

Name That Brings Back a Memory: Timbiriche

Timbiriche is the name of an 80's Mexican pop group
with the likes of Paulina Rubio, Erik Rubin, and Thalia
having been members of it.
>One of the most popular groups from Mexico
>with their music still being
>a significant influence on mainstream pop culture.

They remind me of being a kid, visiting Tía Chuy
and Mama Linda in Reynosa.
>Of the Coca-Cola bottles fresh outta the icebox
>and dulces I could buy for a peso
>from the tiendita near tía's house.

More specifically, Timbiriche reminds me of my flower girl days
and mi primo Pilarin, a teenage noviero
with the hugest celeb crush on Thalia.
>Timbiriche reminds of one particular flower girl dress
>my mother had to put away. Of being seven years old
>and taking a cruise down the streets of Reynosa.

Of being coerced by a handsome primo to sing *Si no es Ahora*.
Of his secret novias I could tell nobody about.
>Of the Gansitos he bribed me with
>so I could ask tía to let him take me de paseo
>when all it was really for
>was to pay a call on a new girlfriend.

The *Quinceañera* song reminds me of his silent goodbyes.
Of the news nobody expected
as we prepared for his sister's wedding.

Timbiriche reminds me of those days
before his mother's forever grief.

        I picture her sitting in her rocking chair
            as she prepared last-minute details for her daughter's wedding.
I hear her impatience, knowing something was wrong
when her son wouldn't come home
as the morning hours passed. I wasn't there
            but I can hear her shrieks when police
            told her of her only son's death.

Timbiriche reminds me of that morning
when instead of a wedding,
we dressed for a funeral.

Carel Ya No Esta

No basta
a billion questions
asked:
>   *¿donde esta?*
>   *¿cuando regresa?*
>   *when did she disappear?*
>   *who's looking for her?*
>   *¿con quien andaba?*
>   *¿en que se involucro?*
>   *was she American?*
>   *do you think she's dead?*
>   *¿y su familia?*

It's quickly done to fit
the same response:
>   *I don't know.*

All I can tell you
with certainty is
>   *Carel ya no esta.*

Of all the billion things
trying to figure themselves out,
that is one thing
for sure.

In this life
of waiting and not knowing,
lo que fue, *fue.*

Nanita's Prayer

feet can carry me forward,
but sideways and backward
sturdies
the fashion of Americanos.
the weapon
is in my accent
when you say
this is where
I come from. sharp
and unfamiliar
to the minds
of resting volcanoes
fitting to the mold
resting for spectators.
bleeding out
the scenery which counts
syllables in my name.

perdónala, mi Dios,
I hear nanita praying
with the herbs
on my tongue
and the rosary
wrapping my fingers.

perdónala. perdónala. perdónala. perdón...
they whisper
when in the mirror
my colors part.

her voice in my voice
when she calls
for an autumn change.

and it is now
I can say
forgive me
in my own tongue.

III

Stories and Heirlooms

"Quien con la esperanza vive, alegre muere."
— popular Mexican dicho

When a Story is an Heirloom

their stories are secrets
scented like a river of lavender water
tell-telling a map of where
        they have been
and flowering as a bouquet
of sequences
now settled in my memory,
        parting me into two –
        that which I know is me
        and that which I figure
        becomes a history of me.
a trace, a bloodline, an inheritance
an atlas
of the worlds before me
and the paths we as an entity
have already taken.

their stories are buried
but never hidden
away in the grating lumber chest
my grandparents
brought home from Reynosa. not every moment
must be so hard
on us
        when the distance
        we traveled
is never far enough
to hide and cry
for fear of belonging. too much to too many.

their stories are rather the worst kind
insisting they have a chance
to exist and re-exist

as they travel
       from one ear out one mouth and into another ear.
so they become
a rather fragile
heirloom needing constant care
and renovations
       from the passing and re-enacting
an aunt, a cousin, a son, a nephew
bring to light
with the recollection another story
has triggered.

their stories are like a trance
we as offspring cannot escape,
whether because we respect our elders
when they tell us a dull chronicle
of childhoods spent out in the labores
       or because we are enchanted
       by the ghosts
       of an old farmhouse in North Dakota.
curative experiences
against blemished ambitions
       and gently ignored
       by our young ignorance
       of appreciating, but not knowing
what we
have never encountered.

their stories are fractures
in our ribs
as we slowly breathe out
the subsistence of our departed
       sangre de sangre
       who come out
rolling the punches
and remembering the relampagos
of their earthly existence,
slowly invading
space only the living
are given credit for.

que en paz descansen
pero
in another cuento,
we resurrect them
from a tomb of hidden memories
that are passed on and on and on
because without them
our heirloom, our family
vanishes
into a steady stream of wondering.

Memories of a Moon Mother

the dirt road between McAllen
and Las Milpas is
as fond a memory
as the Magic Valley's[1] dry current
        bordered by a dancing river.
sugar canes and fields of melon
are scars on my hands
in this silly story -
        might be more memory than truth.
the dusty dirt roads spitting rocks
as we endlessly wandered deserted montes
and a bag of collected cans
slowly took the shape of profit.
Toña telling her stories that mixed
the bible and Aguascalientes,
my brother lagging on one hand
as I gripped the other.
        I never noticed her ropaje then
        as I did when she embarrassed me
        in my teenage years.
Toña is who I see
when I find the strength or when
        she dances and marks my scars.

[1] *In the early 20th century, the Lower Rio Grande Valley was promoted as the Magic Valley by land developers*

tamales for breakfast

with the comal warm enough, Welo throws on
the tamales – corn husk and all.

it took a village to prepare them
takes only two to devour the last dozen.

Welo, which is your favorite tamal?
las más rellenitas.

güerca, and yours?
bean and cheese.

the day is not set, but our evening
of telenovelas and corajes has long been planned.

coffee swirls around the table
pressing its grounds to our ears.

we laugh, shaking our fingers to cool them
after pulling tamales onto our plates.

pero bien tostaditas in their second serving
spreading their warmth inside us.

we sit in silence and wrap our senses
around this small, sheltered world.

McAllen: Our Rinconcito

written for my inauguration as McAllen Poet Laureate

Dancing on bare feet
as I jump into my car, I hear ama
remind me
not to forget the pan dulce
before heading to Wela's house.

KTEX[1] slowly drowns outside noises
as I slip on my chanclas
and Bo Garza's *I'm home*
catches my attention.
I'm home, everybody I'm home.

The air-con on full blast
competing with the 102° heat index
Tim Smith[2] predicted.

¡Ay, que calor!

There's nothing
like a blue coconut raspa
from Young's Snow Wiz
to cool off with
during the Dog Days of summer.

Driving off from my parent's home in McAllen,
the scent of citrus groves
swims in through my car windows.
A quinceañera's baile
drumming tunes from a neighboring dance hall.

De Alba's Bakery is but a moment's drive,

the scent of fresh corn tortillas
and empanadas hitting me as I walk in.
Los Tigres del Norte on the intercom
belting out *Golpes en el Corazón.*
Pero tu que me has dado golpes en el corazón...

Golpes en el corazón
are sometimes the memories
that brought my family closer.

A viejito pays for his tamales
and asks for extra salsita.
With his accent and sombrero,
I cannot help but think of my abuelo.

I slip back into my car
and change the station;
Ramon Ayala y Sus Bravos del Norte
sing about *Un Rinconcito en el Cielo...*

A little piece of heaven
is belonging.

It is listening to cumbias and corridos
while studying at the library.
Knowing the best taquitos
and papas asadas
can be served from a food truck

It is using dichos
and getting your point across.
Being an English speaker
and somehow having a strong 'che' accent.

It is looking forward to the fall
because our Winter Texan[3] friends come home.

This little piece
of heaven is acknowledging your roots
will always hold on.

It is remembering our home
is a community that warms
memories
because it forever embraces us.

This is our rinconcito.

[1]FM 100 KTEX is a Rio Grande Valley (RGV) country music radio station
[2]Chief Meteorologist for KRGV Channel 5 News
[3]During the winter months, seasonal visitors from outside of Texas will escape
harsh weather conditions back home

Jukebox 'Buelita

dedicated to Nana Toña

Estas son las mañanitas
que cantaba doña 'buelita
me las cantaba
me fastidiaba
y nunca hará un por fin.

that was my nana.
my abuelita. thinking
with her heart de oro
and never with her cabeza de mensa.
>   viejitos drooled for her nonsense
>   and the best pumpkin empanadas
>   in the whole entire Valle.

she'd sing me to wake up
with las mañanitas
even when it wasn't my birthday.
or con el canto del gallo…
qui-qui-rri-qui, despertaremos aquí,
qui-qui-rri-qui, qui-qui-rri-qui.

esta loca, my family would say. *¡esta loca!*
y sí, estaba loca.

loca por amar. loca por dar.
loca por conocer. loca por ser. loca por pertenecer.

someday, she'd think, SOME DAY,
Juan Gabriel would discover her
and take her away
to replace the best friend spot
Rocio Durcal had left empty.

No tengo dinero, ni nada que dar.
Lo único que tengo
son empanadas, gorditas, cafecito, y bah.

Mi baybee love, mi baybee love
I want you, oh, I need you…
she sang to the hierbas and plants
growing in her yard
for her curandera remedies.
   Sana, sana, colita de rana
   que se sane hoy y no mañana…
   she'd rub us over and over
   with her lodo that would
   heal our ailments.

La cucaracha, la cucaracha
no se puede levantar. porque
le falta, porque le falta
unas ganas para bailar…
was our song when we were moody
after a nap cut short.

La raspa la baile
con un viejo botijón
y en el medio del salón
se le cayó el pantalón.
Ti-rri-ti-ti-rri, ti-rri-ti-ti,
ti-rri-ti-ti-rri, ti-rri-ti-ti…
for weddings and quinceañeras.

Buelita's hair in the wind
as she waved and she grinned
with her hair free.
A mi me gusta traer el pelo suelto…
   and her fingers twirling a cigarette,
   and her pockets hiding a bottle of tequila.

Mama told me not to come.
She said: That's not the way that it's done,
son. That's not the way that to have fun.

Mocking my father's choice of music
and mocking my interest
       in that chisme to come.

Tequila always brought out the chismes in her.
Borracha and alegre.
I'm so excited y no puedo hide it.
I'm about to lose control...

Buelita, her cigarrillo, and that bottle of tequila
taught me what I know today about heartbreak.

The biggest lesson was when she broke
me away from romance
and taught me to be tough, triumphant. The way
to a man's heart is not always
won over with good manners. It needs style, not class.
And if you have to say
No controles mi forma de pensar
porque es total
y a todos les encanta...
and you need to repeat it more than once,
it's about due time you reevaluate intentions.

But never, never
make a man you love cry
if you can help it.

When we spent more than a weekend apart
her voice would squiggle thru the phone cords
as she'd sing,
Querida-ah-ay, cada momento de mi vida-ah-ah...

Querida is what she was to me.
Buelita. Singing
La del moño colora'o
me trae todo el día borra'o...
to my father
when he had a red lipstick stain
from my mother's kiss.

Dying with laughter
when she was dying in her sleep.
Loving, as always. Singing. Trying
to belt out one last tune…
Y volver, volver, volver
a tus brazos otra vez…

Her voice is gone now.
And in my heart
I can hear her singing
Estas son las mañanitas
que cantaba doña 'buelita
me las cantaba
me fastidiaba
y nunca hará un por fin.

for the pain, Toña took some tequila

her wrists boogied
thus and so to hem
the embroidery of maroon –
fond of the new Mexican earth
on which her indigenous sister produced her youth.
and of callow lime
doting the vegetation
she sowed into the driest clay of Tejas.

asoleada on the porch
she would steal a glance
to her kith and kin
nailing down her refuge
to sneak puffs from a cigarillo.

she'd shiver
under her layers of ropaje
cheapening the roasting
of a hot Indian summer.

she bread rolled
her silver mane
and guaranteed it was
longer than the pasture
across all of El Valle.

her hands wobbled with the arthritis
all those days
of sowing seeds
and mending grins
and turning tortillas
did fee her.

now here's something she would never

let me tell you…
from underneath her apron
she supplied herself
with a tragito
and she sucked
on her bottle.

Ayyy, ¡que alivio! she'd sigh
and bribe me with a fib
of her five husbands.

her mind would sometimes
escape her, and she'd think
I was my mami, her nieta.

a headache meant
she would stare into the nublado
so I made sure
to stand as still as I could
and saw her pretend
she didn't cry.

and again came out the tragito
that was her medicine
and she would croon
to the coyote
only she could set eyes on.

Aiiiiyah. Que destino el mío.

I Remember

The day my primo Eddie was buried with mariachis singing *Un Día a la Vez*.

Chocolate Abuelita with a tinge of canela and a plate of pan de polvo.

I remember days in the sun pointing at rainbows.

The smell of mesquite burning in the distance.

I remember believing.

Connecting with the myth of Gloria Anzaldúa.

I remember being invisible.

Realizing though I am boring, my life really isn't.

Running barefoot in the streets, a tire rolling behind me.

You're out of town and didn't promise to return. Primo, you better return!

Wela te persino before you left, just as she had done for Eddie.

I remember the scent of Wrangler boots is the same as botas from La Pulga[1] in Alamo.

Raspas in the winter and cold fronts in the summer.

I remember fronteras.

I remember to forget borders.

I remember I am a frontera.

[1]An outdoor flea market

It's a Short Piece of Time beneath the Moon's Stare

I begin with an accordion concierto
behind the balcony
leading to a hundred steps
      of smiles and embraces
      and memories reminisced.
I remember with the fable
of abuelo's long lost machete
how time doesn't let us go.

Las penas amargas que a mí me pasan,
croons a drunken uncle
abuela eyes with curiosity.
Es que yo ya no puedo más.

Children run with the measures
of kicks and games
      and adults portray
      the art of chismes
      and the tales they frame.
sometimes ruining a reputation or two.

But the art of molding and the magic of words
can come in many forms.
      a rhyme can commit a crime
      with the context of its expressions
or the offense can create a phantom
one dies to forget.
Es que yo ya no puedo más.

In the arms of her lover,
my aunt promises him eternal devotion -
      not in her own words
      but those of Jose Alfredo Jimenez.

She follows his lead
and my eyes lead me to see
        a wisp of her hair
        perhaps touched by the breath
        of her lover, or the love of the midnight air.
Es que yo ya no puedo más.

Gritos and abrazos
familia y amigos -
we are all the same
beneath the moon's stare.

Manuelito, Meme Bravo

Manuelito lies in his casket
but with his death
is born the strangest revelation.
  His brown face
   worn and ragged by life's short use
   was not the only identity
of a skinny, somewhat wimpy looking man.
most of us, as his family,
were led to think many rumors
I am sure were so and so true.
  His partying, his mano caida, his female fanatics
   his keen sense of loyalty to some secret kept aside.
His disguise was well hidden
with his daytime gig
as costurero de vestidos. Gentle fingers
  softly guiding the seams of a dress behind a sewing machine.
The bruises he occasionally came home with
caused riots
when the thought crossed our minds
the douchebag boyfriend of his
laid a hand too strong on our dear Manuelito.

A veces he came home
with more dineral than a humble
gig or two should have provided - but as it was ignored
  and the subject never brought up, even behind his back,
   we all secretly figured he was in wrong terms with the law.

Manuelito came and went as he pleased - no obligations really
but to provide for his aging mother.
  his clumsy feet
   too often twisting an ankle
   at any given corner of a street.

He dealt without fear of his mortality
as death knocked upon his door
and prepared as we had been
for what we knew was unavoidable,
        no one prepared us for the end of our feared Meme Bravo.

For as we knelt to kiss his cold hands adios
and our eyes swayed to the red mask by his face
the mere recognition and realization
of this ghastly super villain's identity
        was more truth and deception than we had desired.

Manuelito? El Meme Bravo?

For how long had this secret
been kept by his mother? And how dare
        this lucha libre figure insist with his uncovered identity
        we were all related to the worst of worst nightmares!
        Dos de tres caidas for sure
because there is no way
a rudo luchador with no morals
can be our gentle Manuelito!

sometimes things don't change

I sit in my parent's kitchen, taking in the air that makes me homesick for my abuelo's home. I stir sugar into my coffee and stare at the steam rising.

I have done no great things – but I don't think I care much.

sitting here at the dining table listening to Grupo Pesado's *Ayudame a Olvidar*, I forget nothing. life is a spinning wheel of occurrences we fight for and others we run from. r eal life is just so.

real life is not a cliché. It's hardly dependable.

my playlist jumps from ABBA's *SOS* to Chavela's *Albur de Amor*.

Ay, que vida.

Garcia Women

my breath simply finds a way
to swallow me
when Chuyita pays a visit.
we've all said it
before
how when we die
our last hours on earth
won't be in these bodies.

we believe it
we've threatened it
we've knocked on wood
and counted stars
to promise our loved ones
we'll never abandon them.

for five generations
we've parted ways and prayed thru
sleep-deprived nights
with veladoras counting our
sighs and
knuckles gone white.

we've kissed them goodbye
and locked ourselves closed.
but for generations of Garcia women
those apparitions are still there
after us, haunting of presence
when we cannot
comprehend what we fear.

doors closed
and feet entwined

as sisters and nieces
or mothers and daughters
search for sweet dreams.
existing in some realm
amongst evening stars
when sleep would come swiftly
and dread took heed
some other moment.

My Mesquite

my fate sits silently
hanging from a scrawny branch of a mesquite tree -
its unattractive sway in the wind
can describe to you
just who I am
and when the days of my being
begin their countdown to the end.

and just as simple as the color of my brown eyes
are the green edges of those leaves,
hanging by their fingertips
and grasping
to the clouds that escape
from a cold northern breeze.

I feel the calling
sometimes when I cover my eyes
with the doubts of my existence
as it sings a steady cry
I swear I've heard
before my time. Its cry whispers
and leads me on
and forward down a narrow-beaten path
I am not for sure
to be my own. I can feel the tingling
on my skin
as a branch tickles
to guide me away
from the drumbeats
peddled onto a dusty course.

Dreams about Carmen's Cafecito

Carmen gave me one concha for my cafecito
when I specifically and explicitly alleged
to be on a dieta. no sugar for me. no greasy stuff. no extra salt on my beans.
no more fried anything for me.

it's not that I'm really on a diet. Carmen knows well enough
dieting is not in my system right now.
it's that my azucar
is a little too high today.
          but that one concha…that warm cafecito!
damn me for being so weak.
for to me, for to me, for to me
it was too comfortable
in Carmen's old earth kitchen
          and old school talk
          and old, old, old me.

I dream her
and can't recall how she left me
then, or even how her life flashes with such strength.
I cave in…
          I caved, and I can't let go
          of what she has meant.

so comfortable in my memory
a dream
can wake me from the worst.

I go in and around and in and without
a damn doubt
Carmen brews me my weaknesses
and the cafecito
goes with my stories

so I lie about her
and pretend to diet on her death.

a little at a time.
lost a little at a time.
offering me what I hate to taste
what I love to taste – her cafecito
brewing my life.

anillo corriente

for mi Abuelo Eduardo, El Colorín

me pongo este anillo
el brillo ni tan brilloso

es mi estilo corriente
lo que grita al solo perderte

me guía la lastima antigua
que ni existe
tan solo me mira

te escucho
con cada mirada

te oigo
porque todavía no me faltas

te apretó con abrazos
te guardo
costillas de viejo
sonrisas de apio

corriente, corriente, te burlas
antigua Coahuila, me gritas

te escucho
te guardo
te adoro en un comal
te amarro como un costal

palabras Spanglish
cuentos tan raros
chismes extraños

te apretó
te guardo
Colorín Colorado
viejito loco
zapatos apestosos

me dices:
te apretó
te apretó

te guardo
mi antigua Coahuila

sonsa ladeada
con ese anillo de bruja

corriente te crees
pero nunca serás

Las Lloronas sing Baladas and Valses

"Hay más tiempo que vida."
— popular Mexican dicho

It's a
Beautiful
Life

Las Lloronas en el Valle

I.
There are rivers.

South of here, where
borders divide hopes from dreams.

Where el cielo
is overwhelmed with prayers
as they drift, one by ten thousand.

Where tears
flow and never lick their open wounds.

Hope en el otro la'o.

Uprooted. Fear in what is home and
fear in what isn't.

Fear. Wrapped around like una cobija.
A second skin.

II.
There are rivers.

North, where a sanctuary
awaits los del otro la'o.

To track them. Divide them.

Where they learn of
how dreams are stolen.

Mañana.

The distance
becomes ginormous.

III.
There are rivers.

Of tears. Children grasping
in panic at their mother's waist.

Hands. Imprints.

Locked in cages. No embraces, but
the chorus of cries
drowning out their own.

So they drown.

IV.
Mis niños…¿Dónde están mis niños?

Brown mothers with burnt skin search
for their children.

No answers.

Children lost
in a river of separated children.

¿Dónde están mis niños?

La Media Vuelta

te vas por que yo quiero que te vayas
a la hora que yo quiera te detengo
this poem is not a love song
this poem
is not
a call back.

      yo se que mi cariño te hace falta
      por que quieras o no
I'm sorry for cheating you
out of the person
you always deserved to be
but this poem
is not for you.

      te vas por que yo quiero que te vayas
far more than the strain
of your hand against my neck
and I hope
someday I could face you
but for now, I could only pretend.
you see, this is not a love poem.
this is a poem for me.

there is nothing more physical
than the courage it takes
to speak out against you,
the coward I am.
I can try to be a warrior
pero me doy la media vuelta
and doubt my strength.

you see, this is not a love poem.

love would be easy. I've never lied about liking easy.
I know that sounds wrong
but keep in mind, this is a poem for me.

violence seems to be
the only thing free these days.
concern, even from those I love,
comes in the form of *es lo que te pasa por pendeja.*
so little care and so much blame.
        yo se que mi cariño te hace falta

I thought I knew better
but when the only pity I receive
from myself is a pity for being so blind,
how can I pretend?

I've been an advocate against violence
for as long as I can remember and for this
to bring me down so deep, I have so much doubt
y me doy la media vuelta. *WHO* am I?

pendeja. drama. drama.

        te vas por que yo quiero que te vayas
even though I am not dramatic
I am drama.
I wouldn't be surprised if the door flew open
and like a worldly eruption
I found out all my ambitions
were never about me.
isn't that drama?

I'm sorry for cheating myself
out of the luchadora
my double slam arguments could've proven me to be –
but tough, that isn't me.

I'm sorry for ranting and raving
in this poem and I'm sorry
for always being sorry and I'm sorry for

running when I last saw him,
scared he'd see me.

like a stalker almost, but in my case,
I was hiding. I'm a coward.

I should be stronger
but this poem is not to a love poem
for myself. it is merely a poem for me.

> yo se que mi cariño te hace falta
> por que quieras o no
> no tengo dueño

fear is not the boss of me.

I'm sorry I blamed myself
when I thought I took out the worst in you.
for being weaker
than I ever thought I'd be.

Ghosts Don't Get Lost

they maybe take
a wrong turn - not necessarily
by accident.
but ghosts, they don't get lost.
maybe we lose them
when our faith in them
changes - así es la vida.
but ghosts, they don't leave us.
they run around amongst
our kind - sometimes they tickle
and sometimes they hush.
but ghosts, they don't necessarily harm us.
they wrap their great hopes
around our solid arms
as they know us - maybe not in
their life but ours.
but ghosts, they're not like us.
they carry their burdens
and drown in ours
because burdens or not - we
are meant to be lost.
but ghosts, they are.

The Tradition of Silence

for Gloria Anzaldúa

I.
You are the opposite. Maybe you
were different in life when your voice
was more than a myth, it was…it was
more than these translations of words. It was your
voice.
What was your voice like?
Did you sing? *Gloria, you sing to me.*

II.
You are the opposite. You wouldn't know
your songs are fed to me
like spoonfuls of cotton. My tongue swells
with the rhythm of your slashing words.
Gloria, were you always hocicona?
Gloria, were you always repelona?
Gloria, are there chismes you hid?

III.
You are the opposite. Maybe your
saga meant to tame you and your wild
shadow of a myth.

But Gloria, you sing to me.

es más chulo que un ocho

inspired by Sebastian Rulli

so he is. in my opinion,
a little less than el papasote
de Alejandro Fernandez but mas qué
el güero consentido. somehow
his fame is a mix of his smile, his
looks, his grieving tears, his hands
raking those long locks, his tanned arms.

mira, m'ija, mira…¡el desgraciado!

he grabs his novela wife by the arms
and throws her to the floor as she
begs him to believe her. she is innocent!

*la otra pinche vieja anda de metiche y
el menso que se lo cree.*

he warns the innocent wife to vacate
the house within the hour – an impossible
task, if you ask me. he believes the
pinche vieja over his faithful and much
prettier wife? ¡que cabrón!

and then he cries. betrayed –
or so he thinks!

ay, pobrecito…esta llorando.

Dancing on the River
Moon Mother (1)

The woman calls out
as if summoning our dreams
in the moonlight.

Dancing with ghosts
and the spirits
swimming towards the river top.

Dancing on the river
holding her tears.

The banks beneath
hold her feet.

Have so many times
held her clumsy feet.

And the moonlight asks her
to forget those pasts.

A Family Name
Moon Mother (2)

She hears echoes of their names
rolling off her tongue.

Lies she told
to hide their truth.

Children she dreams
were never hers.

Tears she lies
are not her own.

Lies she tells
even after so long.

All of them rolling
off her deceiving tongue.

Dancing
as she drives herself crazy
like those many other times.

Lying to herself
she doesn't remember.

She sees
someone else's nightmare.

Our Rivers that Haunt
Moon Mother (3)

Her cries at night
are a mountain of fear for the mother.
But she has not a desire
other than her own.

Legends fall onto ears of children
while she wails to be forgotten.

No one truly understands
why she waits by rivers
hunting for what no longer exists.
But those moments whistle her to life.

Where could I hide you? she weeps to the wind.
And we know she must have gone crazy.
She weeps to what does not exist.

There is only the wind
and her imagination.

What the Years have Been
Moon Mother (4)

Her ghost, some have said,
does nothing but search for her children.
She died long ago
without longing to hold her back.
I don't know if it is worse
she let her children drown
    or she took her life
    to be rid of that grief.

She drank to the bottom of many bottles.
And still, every night,
she only heard the pleas of her daughters.

This is how it was.

She was stone-blind in her vengeance.
So this is what leads her to become nothing?

Of a Cold Case She Becomes Moon Mother (5)

An old woman
visits the cabin
of a past
    her town became infamous for.
They say
La Llorona's grave itself
is inside those walls.

On many nights
a voice could be heard
weeping
into the many directions
a child can follow.

Cursing like that night
a mother's mind went furious with hate.

The old woman waited
for the weeping woman's ghost to appear.
She heard tales
of La Llorona's ghost
when she was but a girl.

Frightened of this ghost.

She thought of that now.
And how she would always be afraid.

She thought of this now
    as she waited and waited.

Moon Mother's Farewell
Moon Mother (6)

They say she buried
the wind beneath the soil -
it would become her tomb.

And so, it would be that day
she'd make her escape.
Her voice drifting.

But the worst is not her voice
haunting us.

But the songs
she has carried to bellow.

About the Author

Priscilla Celina (Lina) Suárez grew up in the borderlands of South Texas and was the 2015-17 McAllen Poet Laureate, where she had an opportunity to rediscover the many communities in the Rio Grande Valley. During her childhood, she lived surrounded by the farmlands of the then small colonia of Las Milpas, TX, where she first heard many of the leyendas she shares in her book *Cuentos Wela Told Me: That Scared the Beeswax Out of Me.*

Her poetry is a hybrid of rancheras, polkas, pop, rock, and música internacional. A past contributor to the American Library Association's *Young Adult Library Services* magazine, she has previously authored the Texas State Library's *Bilingual Programs Chapter* – allowing her an opportunity to gain experience in writing poetry, rhymes, and tongue twisters for children and teens.

She has shared her poetry in *¡Juventud!: Growing up on the Border* and *Along the River III: Dark Voices from the Río Grande*. In 2003, her work was selected by The Monitor as *The Best Poetry of the Year*. You can learn more about her by visiting her website at www.pcsuarez.com.